Bonsai for Beginners 2022

Discover a Step-By-Step Process To Grow and Take Care of a Bonsai Tree For The First Time.

Copyright © 2022 All rights reserved.

No portion of this book may be reproduced in any form without written permission from the publisher or author, except as permitted by U.S. copyright law.

Under no circumstances will any blame or legal responsibility be held against the publisher, or author, for any damages, reparation, or monetary loss due to the information contained within this book. Either directly or indirectly. You are responsible for your own choices, actions, and results.

Legal Notice:

This book is copyright protected. This book is only for personal use. You cannot amend, distribute, sell, use, quote, or paraphrase any part, or the content within this book, without the consent of the author or publisher.

Disclaimer Notice:

Please note that the information contained within this document is for educational and entertainment purposes only. All effort has been executed to present accurate, up-to-date, reliable, and complete information. No warranties of any kind are declared or implied. Readers acknowledge that the author is not engaging in the rendering of legal, financial, medical, or professional advice. The content within this book has been derived from various sources. Please consult a licensed professional before attempting any techniques outlined in this book.

By reading this document, the reader agrees that under no circumstances is the author responsible for any losses, direct or indirect, which are incurred as a result of the use of the information contained within this document, including, but not limited to, — errors, omissions, or inaccuracies.

Contents

Introduction

1. DEEP ROOTS

    History of the Bonsai

    Art of the Bonsai

2. BONSAI BEGINNINGS

    How Does a Bonsai Tree Work?

    Why Grow a Bonsai Tree at Home?

    A Year in Your Bonsai's Life

    Choosing The Right Tree For You

3. BEST BONSAI TREES FOR BEGINNERS

    Ficus Bonsai

    Juniper Bonsai

    Chinese Elm Bonsai

4. STARTING YOUR BONSAI JOURNEY

- Sourcing the Best Bonsai
- Tools and Equipment
- Creating The Perfect Growing Environment

5. SIMPLE MAINTENANCE TECHNIQUES

- Pot Selection
- Watering
- Fertilizing
- Soil
- Pruning and Trimming
- Wiring
- Repotting
- 9 Top Tips for Ultimate Bonsai Care Mastery

6. COMMON PESTS AND DISEASES, AND HOW TO TREAT THEM

- Aphids
- Scale Insects
- Spider Mites
- Whiteflies
- Mealybugs
- Caterpillars
- Root Rot
- Powdery Mildew

- Bacterial Leaf Scorch
- Fungal Leaf Spot
- Bacterial Blight

7. CREATIVE TRIMMING AND PRUNING

- Formal Upright Style (Chokkan)
- Informal Upright Style (Moyogi)
- Slanting Style (Shakan)
- Cascade Style (Kengai)
- Semi Cascade Style (Han-kengai)
- Literati Style (Bunjingi)
- Broom Style (Hokidachi)
- Windswept Style (Fukinagashi)
- Double Trunk Style (Sokan)
- Multi-trunk Style (Kabudachi)
- Forest Style (Yose-ue)
- Growing on a Rock Style (Seki-joju)
- Raft Style (Ikadabuki)
- Shari Style (Sharimiki)

8. NEXT LEVEL BONSAI

- Summer Care
- 11 Advanced Techniques for the Bonsai Gardener

5 Beginner Mistakes to Avoid

9. FREQUENTLY ASKED QUESTIONS

Conclusion

Resources

Introduction

As a child, I visited my grandparents' home in the countryside of Japan every summer. My grandfather was a keen gardener, and I would often help him tend to his herb garden. One summer, he showed me how he grew and cared for his treasured bonsai trees. They were the most beautiful trees I had ever seen. I fell in love with their beauty as the summer warmth filled the air that year.

My grandfather explained that these miniature trees were unique because they could be kept small and delicate through careful pruning. After that summer, my fascination with bonsai grew, and I would often help my grandfather care for his trees.

I yearned year after year to return to my grandfather's side and continue learning the secrets he had learned from his father many decades before. I know that my grandfather also enjoyed spending time with me and teaching me the art of bonsai, even though he never voiced his pleasure in doing so.

As I grew older, I found myself continually drawn by my fascination with gardening, particularly the meditative art of cultivating the bonsai. I moved to another prefecture of Japan to study gardening. I eventually started my business growing and selling bonsai trees. I loved working with these beautiful plants and sharing my passion with others.

One day, an elderly gentleman came into my shop and asked to buy a bonsai tree. I could tell he was an experienced gardener, so I showed him the best trees in my collection. The man chose a small juniper bonsai and told me how he had been growing bonsai trees for over 50 years. I was amazed by his knowledge and skill.

Over the years, I have continued to learn from the old gentleman, and he has become a dear friend and a mentor to me. He has taught me the importance of patience and care when growing bonsai trees. I am grateful that I have been able to follow my passion for gardening, and I hope to continue growing beautiful bonsai trees for many years to come.

I have written this book hoping that I can show my readers the incredible joy one can experience when growing and caring for bonsai trees. I hope you enjoy reading this book as much as I have enjoyed writing it.

In this book, I will discuss the basics of growing bonsai trees. I will explain how to select the right tree, care for it, and style it in your unique way.

So if you are interested in learning about this fascinating art form, please keep reading. Bonsai for Beginners is a comprehensive guide that will teach you everything you need to know about growing these plants of great beauty.

Chapter One

DEEP ROOTS

History of the Bonsai

Bonsai (盆栽, "tray planting" or "pot plant") is the Japanese art form of growing an ornamental, dwarf tree or shrub in a container. Bonsais are not genetically manipulated dwarf plants. Instead, they are regular trees and shrubs that have been artificially dwarfed through selective pruning of roots and shoots and pinching and wiring of new growth.

This ancient practice originated in China, where it was known as "penjing," and was introduced to Japan in the 6th century. The bonsai tree symbolizes peace and harmony and has been around for centuries.

Bonsai trees were initially used to teach monks about patience and humility. Bonsai can be traced back to the Tang Dynasty (618-907 AD), when they were used as ornamental plants in the imperial palace. In subsequent centuries, the art of bonsai flourished, and many famous trees were grown and displayed at various botanical gardens and temples. The Japanese began cultivating bonsai during the Kamakura period (1185-1333), and the art form soon became popular among the samurai class.

One of the most renowned bonsai trees is the Yamaki Pine. Almost 400 years old, the Japanese white pine survived the bombings of Hiroshima. It is a testament to the art of bonsai that such an ancient tree has been able to survive for centuries in a small pot. The Yamaki Pine was gifted to the United States in 1976 as Japan's bicentennial gift to the American people and is now on display at the National Bonsai and Penjing Museum in Washington, D.C.

The popularity of bonsai continued to grow in the 20th century, and the first international bonsai show was held in London in 1936. Today, bonsai trees are cultivated worldwide, and many different styles have been developed.

The most common type of bonsai is the "informal upright," which features a trunk that curves gently upwards. The informal upright bonsai tree is considered the most challenging style to grow, but it is also the most popular.

Art of the Bonsai

Bonsai is a horticultural art form that involves cultivating and shaping small trees or shrubs. Trees are traditionally grown from seedlings or cuttings, and they are carefully pruned and shaped to create an aesthetically pleasing miniaturized tree. The bonsai artist strives to create harmony between the tree, the pot, and the overall composition.

Bonsai aims to create a miniature tree that resembles a full-sized specimen in shape and size. Bonsai artists use several techniques to shape the tree, including pruning, wiring, and potting. Bonsai can be grown from seeds, cuttings, or grafting. The most popular species for bonsai are Juniper, Maple, and Elm.

Bonsai is a living work of art that requires patience, skill, and dedication. To create a beautiful and healthy bonsai tree, the experienced bonsai artist must understand plant anatomy and horticultural principles.

There are many different styles of bonsai, each with its unique aesthetic. The most popular types are formal upright, informal upright, slanting, cascade, semi-cascade, literati, and broom. Bonsai can be displayed indoors or outdoors.

The formal upright style is the most traditional style of bonsai. With this style, the tree has a straight trunk and symmetrical branches. The informal upright style is more natural and asymmetrical than the formal upright style. The slanting style is similar to the informal upright style, but the trunk leans to one side. The cascade style features a tree trained to grow downward over a pot, while the semi-cascade type has a trained tree to grow partially over a pot. The literati style is characterized by a thin, slim trunk and sparse foliage. The broom style features a tree that is trained to grow horizontally.

To help you choose which style appeals to your bonsai journey, I will go through these styles in greater depth in a later chapter.

Bonsai can be enjoyed for its aesthetic beauty, but it also has many practical applications. Bonsai trees are used in meditation and therapy, and they can be beneficial for people with ADHD and autism. Bonsai trees are also used in landscaping to add beauty and interest to a garden.

Bonsai is a beautiful art form that requires patience, skill, and dedication. Crafting the bonsai is a meditative journey.

Chapter Two

BONSAI BEGINNINGS

How Does a Bonsai Tree Work?

Bonsai trees are fascinating and beautiful works of art. But how do they work? How can such intricate and detailed designs be created using only a tree?

The simple answer is that bonsai trees are created through careful cultivation and training. This process begins with the selection of a suitable tree species. The tree is then grown in a small pot, using techniques that encourage it to grow in a compact and stylized form.

The life cycle of a bonsai tree is divided into three phases: the seedling phase, the development phase, and the refinement phase.

In the seedling phase, the tree is young and growing rapidly. The goal during this phase is to create a solid and healthy tree that will be the foundation for the future bonsai.

The tree's growth is controlled and directed through pruning, wiring, and other techniques during the development phase. The basic shape of the bonsai is established during this phase.

The bonsai is carefully sculpted into its final form in the refinement phase. The tree is trimmed and shaped to create the desired effect, and the details are added that make the bonsai genuinely unique.

Bonsai trees are living works of art that require a lifetime of care and attention. But the rewards of owning a bonsai are well worth the effort. These beautiful trees are a source of pride and enjoyment for their owners and fascination for everyone who sees them.

Why Grow a Bonsai Tree at Home?

The popularity of bonsai trees has exploded in recent years, and for a good reason. These beautiful, miniature trees can add a touch of natural elegance to any home. But what is it about bonsai that has people so captivated?

Growing your bonsai tree is a great way to connect with nature. Bonsai trees are miniature versions of natural trees and require the same care and attention as their full-sized counterparts. By caring for a bonsai tree, you learn about the delicate balance between plants and their environment.

Bonsai trees are also incredibly versatile. Whether you want a traditional tree shape or something more abstract, you can create it with bonsai. You can achieve dozens of different styles with a bonsai tree, and your imagination only limits the possibilities.

Of course, one of the most appealing aspects of bonsai trees is their size. Because they're small, bonsai trees can be grown indoors – making them the perfect addition to any home.

Bonsais are not only beautiful, but they can also be great for your health. Studies have shown that having plants in your home can help to improve air quality and reduce stress levels. Bonsais are also known to boost moods and create a sense of calm in those who care for them.

If you're thinking about growing your bonsai tree, there are a few things you should know first. This guide will show you everything you need to start, from choosing the right tree to caring for it properly.

A Year in Your Bonsai's Life

Bonsai trees are living, growing things. They experience the full force of the seasons just like any other tree or plant. As a bonsai grower, you can shape and influence your tree's growth in profound ways - ways that wouldn't be possible if you left it to grow in the wild.

The first thing to understand is that trees are influenced by two main factors: temperature and light. Temperature determines how fast a tree grows, while light determines the direction of that growth.

As the days get longer in the spring and the temperatures begin to rise, your bonsai will grow more rapidly. The extra light and warmth stimulate the tree's metabolism, causing it to produce more leaves and branches. This is when you should be pruning your tree heavily to direct the new growth in the desired direction.

As summer approaches and the temperatures continue to rise, the growth of your bonsai will slow down as the tree enters its dormant period. This is an important time for rest and recovery, so don't do any significant pruning during this time.

The reduced light and warmth signal the tree that it's time to start preparing for winter when growth will almost halt. As the days get shorter and the temperatures drop, your bonsai's growth will slow down in the fall. This is when you should be doing your final pruning to shape the tree for the coming winter.

Finally, in winter, the tree will enter a complete state of dormancy, during which little or no growth will occur. This is an important time for the tree to rest and rebuild its energy reserves, so don't do any pruning or styling during this time.

As you can see, by understanding the seasons and how they influence your bonsai, you can profoundly impact the tree's growth and shape. By shaping and pruning at the correct times of the year, you can create a healthy tree that will live for many years.

Choosing The Right Tree For You

The first step in growing your bonsai tree is choosing the right tree. There are a few things you'll need to take into consideration when making your selection, including:

The size of the tree. Bonsai trees come in all different sizes, from tiny trees that can fit in the palm of your hand to larger trees that stand several feet tall. It's essential to choose a tree proportional to your available space.

The type of tree. Many different trees can be used for bonsai, including evergreens, deciduous trees, and fruit trees. Each type of tree has its unique characteristics, so it's essential to choose one that fits your aesthetic preferences.

The tree's age. Bonsai trees can be either young or old. Younger trees are typically easier to care for, but they may not have the same aesthetic appeal as an older tree. It's up to you to decide which is more important to you.

Chapter Three

BEST BONSAI TREES FOR BEGINNERS

When just starting, it's best to choose a tree species based on your growing space and experience level. If you're looking for a bonsai to grow indoors, the **Ficus Bonsai** is ideal for beginners. If you have an outdoor space picked for your first bonsai, then the **Juniper Bonsai** is perfect. A third and prevalent option is the **Chinese Elm Bonsai**, a versatile tree that can be grown both inside and outside. We will now cover specific guidelines for these three trees. However, general care maintenance will be discussed in greater detail in a later chapter.

Ficus Bonsai

The Ficus Bonsai is an excellent choice for beginners because it is an easy-to-care-for tree that can be grown indoors. This species is a member of the Ficus family and is native to the tropical regions of Asia. The Focus Bonsai has attractive green leaves and a sturdy trunk. It can grow up to 12 inches tall and is ideal for small spaces.

Placement

The Ficus Bonsai should be placed in a bright, sunny spot and kept in relatively consistent temperatures. It can be taken outside during the summer months; however, it should be brought back inside when temperatures drop below 50 °F (10 °C).

Watering

The Ficus Bonsai should be watered regularly, but be careful not to overwater. Allow the soil to dry out slightly between waterings, but not completely.

Fertilizing

Fertilize this species every two weeks during the summer season with a water-soluble fertilizer and every four weeks during the winter if the tree continues to grow. Liquid fertilizer and organic fertilizer pellets can be used.

Pruning and Trimming

Regular pruning is necessary to maintain the shape of the Ficus Bonsai. Prune after new growth appears, typically in the spring. Prune back to one-third of the new development. Trimming can be done with good-quality scissors; however, sterilize them before using them.

Wiring

The Ficus can be wired to shape it as you desire. Begin by gently shaping the tree and then wrapping the wire around two branches with the same piece of wire and fanning them out gently. When opened up, these trees grow best, so keep this in mind when shaping the branches. Check the wire regularly to ensure it is not cutting into the bark.

Repotting

The Ficus Bonsai should be repotted every two to three years. Use a well-draining potting mix, such as cactus mix or bonsai mix. Be sure to choose a pot about 2/3 in length to that of the tree's height.

Pests and Diseases

The Ficus Bonsai is a sturdy tree and is not typically affected by pests or diseases. Dry air and a lack of light can often weaken the Ficus tree's immune system and lead to an infestation of pests. However, watch for aphids, mealybugs, and scale. If these pests are detected, they can be removed with horticultural oil or insecticidal soap.

Juniper Bonsai

If you're looking for an outdoor bonsai tree, the Juniper Bonsai is excellent. This species is native to temperate regions of the Northern Hemisphere and can tolerate a range of climates, from cold winters to hot summers. Juniper Bonsais have green needles and grow up to 36 inches tall. They are relatively easy to care for and make a beautiful addition to any outdoor space.

Placement

Your Juniper bonsai should be placed outdoors in a spot that receives full sun. If you live in a climate with hot summers, it's essential to ensure your tree is shaded from the sun during the hottest part of the day. Protect your Juniper bonsai from frost during the winter by placing it in a sheltered location.

Watering

Juniper Bonsais prefer to be watered regularly, but not constantly. During the summer, water your tree every other day. In the winter, water it once a week. Be sure to water the tree deeply until the soil is moist but not wet.

Fertilizing

Fertilize your Juniper bonsai every two weeks during the growing season using organic fertilizer pellets. Using higher nitrogen levels during the spring will help promote new growth.

Pruning and Trimming

Prune your Juniper bonsai in late winter or early spring before new growth begins. Cut back the branches to shape the tree and remove any dead or damaged branches.

Wiring

Juniper bonsais can be wired to help shape them into the desired form. Use soft wire, as Juniper needles are delicate and can be easily damaged. The wire should only be left in place for a few weeks.

Repotting

Repot your Juniper bonsai every two to three years, in early spring. Choose a pot about 2/3 in length to the tree's height. Be sure to use well-draining bonsai soil.

Pests and Diseases

Juniper Bonsais are resistant to pests and diseases but watch for aphids, mealybugs, and scale. If these pests are detected, they can be removed with horticultural oil or insecticidal soap. Pests can be controlled with regular applications of neem oil. Brown needles on the Juniper Bonsai may be a sign of spider mites.

Chinese Elm Bonsai

The Chinese Elm is native to China and south-east Asia. It can be a massive tree in its natural habitat, growing up to 80 feet tall (25 meters). Because it has small leaves and fine branch ramification, it makes an excellent Bonsai plant.

Placement

The Chinese elm tree will grow in either full sun or partial shade. In the winter, it may be kept outside even in cold climates. If you have an indoor Chinese Elm Bonsai, you can place it outside during the summer; however, it's best to bring it into a cool but frost-free room during the winter. The Chinese Elm is a hardy tree that can survive some frost, but it varies depending on where it was imported from. Trees from northern regions of China are more frost-hardy than those from southern areas. The leaves of Chinese Elms drop or remain dormant in the winter when the new shoots emerge, depending on the severity of the weather.

Watering

The Chinese Elm does not endure prolonged drought or continual wetness. Wait until the soil is dry before watering, and water generously to ensure that all of the root mass is moistened.

Fertilizing

During the growing season, feed your Chinese Elm with lots of fertilizer. You don't need to use any expensive fertilizers. A mix of solid organic fertilizer and a well-balanced liquid chemical fertilizer works wonderfully. No fertilization is required when the elm tree is dormant during the winter.

Pruning and Trimming

The Chinese Elm thickens quickly and requires frequent trimming to produce a dense network of fine branches. Before cutting it back, allow the branch to develop 3 or 4 additional nodes before pruning back to 1 - 2 leaves. After significant pruning, the tree's buds thrive. Late fall is when you should prune larger branches most effectively.

Wiring

The Chinese Elm is a wonderful tree to work with when utilizing standard wire and guy wire methods.

Repotting

When Chinese Elm trees are young, they should be repotted every two years. They can be repotted less often as they get older and more extensive. Spring is the best time to repot elms, regardless of their age. The roots of elms become twisted and entangled, so it's critical to execute root pruning with care and precision to create a beautiful nebari. It doesn't require any particular soil type, but it's preferable if well-draining. A basic soil mix will suffice.

Pests and Diseases

When the humidity level is low, the Chinese Elm is frequently infested by spider mites or scale. Pesticides should be used correctly, and frequent water spraying helps to prevent pests and illnesses. Avoid using thinned lime-sulfur or systemic pesticides since this may cause the Chinese Elm to shed all of its leaves.

Chapter Four

STARTING YOUR BONSAI JOURNEY

Sourcing the Best Bonsai

When it comes to finding the best beginner bonsai trees, you have a few different options. You can purchase a tree from a local nursery or garden center, an online bonsai retailer, or a specialty bonsai store.

Local Nursery or Garden Center: If you have a local nursery or garden center, they may sell bonsai trees. This is an excellent option if you want to see the tree before purchasing it.

Online from a Bonsai Retailer: Many online retailers sell bonsai trees, and a great option if you want to see a wide variety of trees before choosing one.

Specialty Bonsai Store: If you live in an area with a specialty bonsai store, they will have a large selection of bonsai trees and all the supplies and tools you need to care for your tree. This is an excellent option if you want to purchase everything you need in one place.

Choose a reputable retailer when you are ready to purchase your first bonsai tree. This will ensure that you get a healthy tree that will thrive in your home.

Checking Health

Before bonsai reach the point of sale, they have often spent months, or years, waiting to be bought. As a result, many bonsai suffer stress and ailments due to this long period of neglected care.

For this reason, if possible, you should check the bonsai tree you plan to buy from the bottom up to ensure you are starting your bonsai journey with a tree that has the best chance of survival, a tree that will thrive in your care.

Methods for Checking Health

- Gently rock the tree trunk back and forth to see if the tree is grounded in its pot. If it rocks effortlessly, the roots may not be filling the pot. Movement may indicate that the roots are rotting or not growing well.

Check the pot drainage holes and ensure that roots are not blocking them. If moss is growing over the soil, this is a good sign.

- Check for old wounds that may not have been appropriately sealed. Untreated wounds may cause further complications for you in the future, so it is best to avoid trees with this issue.
- Yellowing leaves can mean under or over watering, inadequate light, or a lack of trace elements, particularly magnesium. Yellow leaves may also point to more severe root issues, so the trunk rocking test should be carried out to determine this.
- Dry foliage areas may be caused by inadequate watering or spider mite infestations.

If you notice any of the issues above when choosing your bonsai, discuss this with the nursery staff, or avoid buying trees with these issues altogether. Buying a healthy tree is one of the most important first steps in bonsai care, as it ensures you have a good foundation for a lasting, happy and healthy bonsai.

Tools and Equipment

Now that you've chosen the perfect tree for your first bonsai, it's time to gather the tools and equipment you'll need to get started. Bonsai cultivation is a relatively simple process, but some essential tools and supplies are necessary to keep your tree healthy and looking its best.

As a beginner, keep things simple and don't invest in many tools until you need to. Below is a list of the must-have tools and equipment for anyone embarking on the bonsai journey. These tools are more than sufficient to get you started:

Bonsai Pruning Tools: These are specially designed to cut through small branches and leaves without damaging the tree. A good quality set of **pruning shears, concave cutters (8-inch cutters are the best), scissors, and wire cutters** are essential for proper trimming and pruning.

Bonsai Wire: Bonsai wire is used to shape and style the branches of your tree. Bonsai trees require two types of wire: **anodized aluminum** and **annealed copper**. Aluminum wire is preferable for deciduous plants, while the more rigid copper wire is better for conifers and pines. I recommend using anodized aluminum wire if you're just starting out, as it's easier to work with and manipulate around small branches. 1.0- 2.0-, and 3.0- millimeter gauge wire works best.

Watering Can: A watering can with a fine nozzle is the best way to water your bonsai tree, to get to those tight spaces under your tree, and prevent the soil from washing away when watering. Choose a lightweight watering can with a large top opening for easy filling.

Gardening/Medical Gloves: These are optional; however, gloves will protect your hands from cuts and scratches while working with your bonsai tree if that's a concern you may have. Thin gloves are best as they allow you to feel the delicate details of the tree's branches while tending to your tree.

Cut Paste: Grey wound sealing paste is used to seal cuts when pruning.

Chopsticks/Root Hook: Chopsticks or a root hook work equally well for targeted pruning, and they are an essential tool in your arsenal. Teasing old soil from the root ball, then untangling delicate roots before root trimming and tree repotting is more manageable with chopsticks or a root hook.

Jacking/Bending Tool: This tool allows drastic changes to the tree's structure to be achieved. When working with thick branches, a jacking tool can come in handy for this purpose. These come in a variety of sizes, however, the smallest size works well for a beginner.

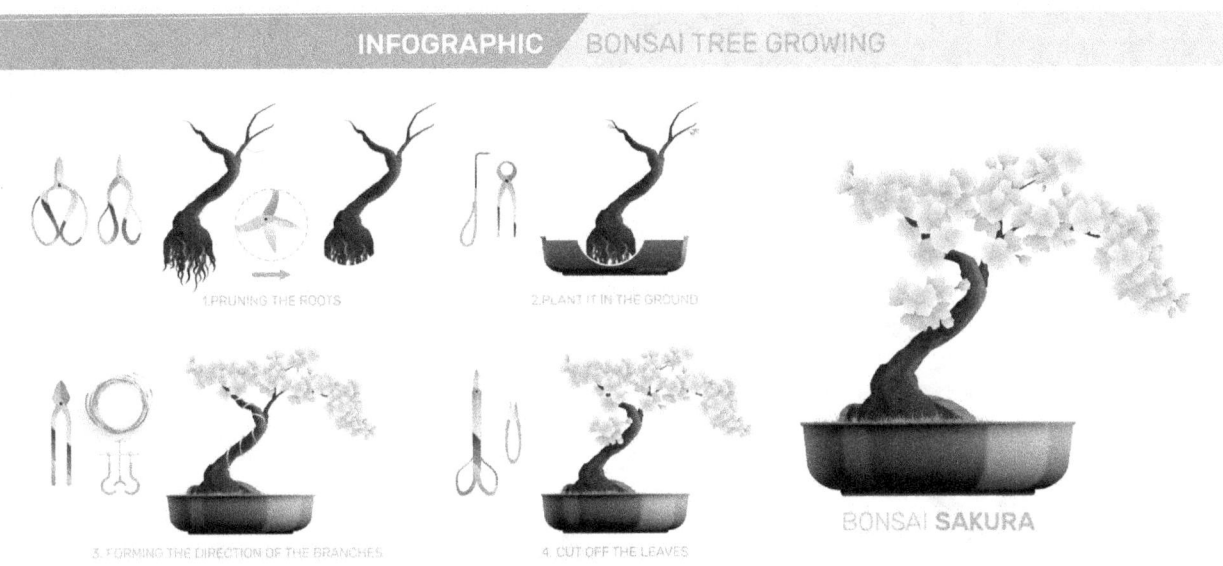

Illustration 1.0 clearly shows the relationship between your tools and at which stage of bonsai care they are used. 1. Bonsai shears are used to trim the downward/vertical roots prior to repotting. This encourages outward growth of the root system, creating a Nebari. 2. The use of chopsticks or a root hook (pictured) are used to tease away old soil from the roots, and untangle roots prior to repotting. 3. Wire, wire cutters and/or a jacking tool are used to shape your bonsai when conducting structural pruning, gently bending branches to create an appealing style. 4. Bonsai scissors are used to

cut the leaves and small branches of your bonsai to complete the pruning and styling process.

Creating The Perfect Growing Environment

Now that you have all the tools and equipment you'll need, it's time to create the perfect growing environment. This includes creating a proper climate for your tree.

Indoor Placement

Placement is so crucial for the health of a bonsai. Inside, trees should be placed directly in front of a south-facing window, but not too close. Don't keep your tree on the windowsill as the cold emitted from the window during the night may shock the tree. This is the only way they will receive enough sunlight to stay healthy. If you don't have a south-facing window, you can place your tree under grow lights.

Indoor bonsai are usually of the subtropical or tropical variety, as these trees are more tolerant of the lower light levels found indoors. Because of this, they need to live in a relatively high humidity environment to stay healthy; between 40 – 60% humidity is ideal. One way to increase the humidity level is to place the pot on a tray of wet pebbles. The water will evaporate and create a humid environment around the trees. A small humidifier can also be used in the room your bonsai lives.

Outdoor Placement

The first step is to choose the perfect location for your tree. Bonsai trees need lots of sunlight, so choose a spot in your garden or inside space that receives full sun, at least 6 hours per day. If you live in a climate with hot summers, you may need to provide some afternoon shade for your tree.

First, make sure that the climate is suitable for your tree. Some trees can only live in certain climates and will die if moved outside of their natural environment. Second, consider your tree's size. A small bonsai will not do well in direct sun all day long and may need to be moved to a shaded area during the hottest part of the day.

Once you've chosen the perfect spot, it's time to prepare the area for your bonsai tree. If planting outside in your garden, begin by removing any weeds or grass from the site. Then, use a garden trowel to dig a hole approximately twice the depth and diameter of the tree's root ball. Place the tree in the hole with new compost, fill gaps with fresh compost, firm down, and water. A good quality organic compost works wonders for the tree as the fibrous content holds water well but still allows water to drain from the tree's roots to maintain healthy moisture levels.

Now that your bonsai tree has a home, it's time to start caring for it.

Chapter Five

SIMPLE MAINTENANCE TECHNIQUES

Pot Selection

Your bonsai tree's health is always the most important when selecting the right pot. A finished bonsai has often undergone years of refinement, so choosing the right pot is paramount. It should be large enough to accommodate the tree's roots but not so large that it looks out of proportion. A general rule of thumb is to find a pot about 2/3 in length to that of the tree's height. The pot should also have drainage holes to allow water drainage and aeration.

Masculine or Feminine

When choosing a pot, the aesthetics and energy of the tree need to be represented by the pot. For example, a masculine tree requires a masculine pot to support and enhance its display of strength and power. A feminine tree needs a more delicate pot to reflect its more graceful beauty. The grace, smooth bark, sparse branches, and curves of a feminine tree would look best in an oval or round planter. In general, the sharp angles, rough bark, and dense foliage of a male tree look best in a squared or rectangular pot.

Size

A general rule is that the pot should be of the same width as the trunk's height above the Surface roots (Nebari). Oval and rectangular pots are the most popular shapes, but square pots are also used. The pot must have drainage holes in the bottom and a wire mesh screen or filter to keep the soil from washing out.

The size of the tree is also essential when choosing a pot. Young trees should be potted in small containers, while larger specimens require larger pots. As the tree matures, it will need a proportionate pot to its size.

Design

As mentioned above, the pot's design should match your tree's degree of masculinity or femininity. The closer you get, the more harmonious and pleasing the combination will be. There are three schools of design that pots may fall into: formal, informal, and naturalistic.

Formal pots have a more geometric shape with clean lines and symmetry. They often have a single or dominant feature, such as a large lip or handle. Informal pots are less structured and more free-form, featuring curves and soft lines. Naturalistic pots are the most realistic, resembling objects in rural settings such as baskets, bowls, or urns.

The pot's design should also match the theme of your bonsai display. If you use a formal pot, your tree should have a formal style. If you use an informal pot, your tree should have an informal style. The same is true for naturalistic pots and trees.

Watering

Bonsai trees need to be watered regularly, as they have a shallow root system that dries out quickly. The watering frequency will depend on the type of tree, the size of the pot, the climate, and the time of year. Be sure to check the soil regularly and water when it is dry to the touch. It's best to water your tree using a watering can with a fine nozzle to get to those tight spaces under the tree and prevent soil from being washed away. As for humidity, most trees prefer a relative humidity of 40-60%.

Watering your bonsai tree is essential, but it is also easy to overdo it. This is a valuable method that my grandfather taught me all those years ago when determining moisture content, and it is simple to do;

Grab a handful of soil and squeeze it in your fist. If the soil stays in a clump and doesn't crumble when you open your hand, then it's too wet. If the soil falls apart in your hand and feels dry, then it's too dry. If the soil holds together in a clump but feels moist, it's suitable for your bonsai.

Knowing when to water will become more evident with experience. If it's an inside tree, you can take your tree and place it in the kitchen sink to water thoroughly without creating a mess. Another method is to stick your finger into the soil 0.4"; water the tree if the soil is slightly dry.

Automated Watering Systems - Blumat and Gardena Microdrip

An automated watering system is another option for watering your bonsai with peace of mind, although it can be costly. These systems are helpful when you're on vacation or for times when you can't physically water your tree. It may be necessary to water your tree twice a day in the summer months. There are a few different systems to choose from – I recommend looking at the **Blumat** or **Gardena Microdrip** for this watering solution if you find it difficult to tend to your bonsai daily.

These systems have their limitations, so be sure to research both systems carefully before purchasing. For instance, if you're going on vacation and your tree will be left unattended for more than a week, it's best to have someone check on it and water as needed, even with an automated system in place.

Fertilizing

Bonsai trees need to be fertilized regularly to stay healthy. I recommend using a fertilizer made specifically for bonsai trees. There are three essential elements in any fertilizer; Nitrogen, Phosphorous, and Potassium (NPK.) Nitrogen increases the growth of leaves and green shoots, Phosphorous helps with root development, and Potassium helps with overall health and disease resistance. Be sure to follow the instructions on the fertilizer package for application rates.

Many growers use different ratios of NPK for different trees and at other times of the year. However, experts increasingly recommend using the same NPK ratio throughout the Bonsai growth cycle, which is a fertilizer called 10-10-10. 10-10-10 stands for the percentage of NPK found in the fertilizer, 10% Nitrogen, 10% Phosphorous, and 10% Potassium. 10-10-10 is considered a complete fertilizer because it consists of the primary nutrients.

When using 10-10-10, I strongly recommend using it at half strength with every watering during the growing season. I have seen fantastic results with my own bonsai using it in this way. Alternatively, many experts recommend using organic fertilizer as it decomposes and releases the nutrients slowly over time.

Most Bonsai trees should be fertilized during the growing season, early spring through mid-fall. Older and more mature trees may only need to be occasionally fertilized depending on their size and health. Indoor trees can be fertilized year-round, but don't overdo the amount of fertilizer used. Be sure to wash any excess off of the leaves to prevent burning.

Soil

Bonsai soil is an essential part of your tree's care. Good bonsai soil should be able to hold moisture and nutrients while still draining well. It's also vital that the soil can support root growth.

There are many types of soil available on the market, and it can be unclear which one is best for your tree. A good rule of thumb is to use a well-draining soil mix made explicitly for bonsai trees. You can find pre-mixed soils at your local nursery or create your own mix by combining potting soil, sand, and organic matter.

One of the most important aspects of bonsai soil is the ratio of organic matter to the soil. Organic matter helps the soil to hold moisture and nutrients, while the sand helps to drain well. The general mix ratio is two parts organic matter to one part sand.

Soil Quality

The soil requires several qualities for it to be considered a good soil mix for your bonsai:
- It should be loose and airy to allow the roots to spread easily
- It should hold moisture well without being waterlogged
- It should drain well to avoid root rot
- It should be rich in nutrients to support growth
- It should be free of pests and diseases

Organic or Inorganic Soils

There are two types of soils available for bonsai: organic and inorganic.

Organic soils are made up of materials from the earth, such as potting soil, compost, and manure. Inorganic soils are made up of materials that do not come from the earth, such as sand, perlite, and vermiculite.

If choosing organic soils, I recommend using a type that contains pine bark, as it helps to improve drainage. Inorganic soils are often considered the best soil for bonsai because they drain well and are less likely to cause root rot, but they do not contain as many nutrients as organic soils.

It is important to note that bonsai trees can use either type of soil; it is just a matter of personal preference. Many people find that organic soils are easier to work with, while others prefer inorganic soils' durability and draining qualities.

Soil Components

- **Akadama** is one of the best soil types for bonsai. Akadama is an inorganic soil made of red clay and used by many bonsai growers. It is suitable for bonsai because it drains well and holds nutrients. Although expensive in many Western countries, experienced enthusiasts use Akadama soil due to its unique properties, using it by itself, or mixing it with sand for pines and species adapted to drought.
- **Pumice** is another type of inorganic soil made up of volcanic ash. It is also a good soil for bonsai because it is lightweight, drains well, and holds nutrients.
- **Organic matter** is an essential component of any soil mix for bonsai. The most common organic matter used is compost, but you can also use peat moss, bark, or leaf mold. However, on its own, it retains too much moisture and doesn't drain well, so it is essential to mix it with inorganic materials such as sand or perlite.
- **Lava rock** is a type of inorganic soil made up of volcanic rock. It is a good soil for bonsai because it drains well and is lightweight.
- **Sand** is a type of inorganic soil made up of tiny rock particles. It is a

good soil for bonsai because it drains well and is cheap.

- **Perlite** is a type of inorganic soil made up of volcanic glass. It is often used in bonsai soil because it is lightweight, helps to aerate the soil, and holds moisture.
- **Vermiculite** is a type of inorganic soil that is made up of mica. It is often used in bonsai soil because it is lightweight, helps to aerate the soil, and holds moisture.

Recommended Bonsai Soil Mixtures

Here are two soil mixtures that I use and recommend, depending on your bonsai tree species:

Deciduous Bonsai soil: 2 parts Akadama, 1 part pumice

Conifer Bonsai soil: 2 parts Akadama, 1 part lava rock

When mixing these soils, it is vital to use a soil mix specifically for bonsai. Regular potting soil or garden soil is too dense and doesn't drain well, which can lead to root rot.

It is also important to note that the ratios above are a general guide, and you may need to adjust the proportions depending on the specific needs of your bonsai tree.

Pruning and Trimming

Pruning and trimming are essential parts of bonsai tree care, as they help shape and style the tree. Bonsai pruning tools are specially designed to cut through small branches and leaves without damaging the tree.

There are two main types of pruning; **structural pruning** and **maintenance pruning**. Structural pruning is done when the tree is relatively young and is used to shape the overall form of the tree, allowing you to control the direction of new growth.

Structural pruning aims to achieve a natural look for your bonsai tree, as seen in nature.

Structural Pruning For Your Bonsai:

Begin by learning about basic bonsai styles - formal upright, informal upright, slant, cascading, multi-trunk, or windswept - and deciding which best fits your plant. Take care with this step and think about your overall vision because it will define the primary form of the trunk and major branches. Remember that structural pruning takes time, often many years, so keeping an ultimate vision in mind will help keep you focused.

Follow These Steps in Early Spring:

Before starting:

1. Make sure your tools are clean and sharp, as this will ensure a clean cut and reduce the chance of harming your tree.
2. Place the tree so that it is at eye level and look at it from all sides.
3. Choose the trunk front (the side of the trunk that will always be viewed).
4. Remove all of the dead branches from the tree first.

5. Examine your tree closely and determine which branches need to be cut to create the desired design.

Designing a tree is more of an artistic activity than one governed by 'rules.' Take a look at the Creative Trimming and Pruning chapter for style guides.

Pruning Branches

Pruning bonsai branches is a reasonably straightforward process that requires slightly more care and attention than pruning a regular garden plant. Because bonsai trees are smaller in structure, healing tissues can form wound swelling and ugly scarring that would otherwise disappear on a garden shrub. Following these steps will eliminate this issue:

Always prune in late winter or early spring, when the tree is most active, and healing begins immediately.

1. Cut the branch as close to the trunk as possible without damaging the bark on the trunk and using sharp concave cutters.
2. Once the cut has been made, use a modeling knife with a curved blade to hollow out the wound, and work from the outside inwards. Once the edge of the wound is flush with the trunk, move on to the next step.
3. Continue carving out the cavity until it is two to three annual rings deep. Carving ensures that during the healing process, the new tissue fills the cavity from the wound's circumference and fills the wound, leaving it flush with the surrounding bark.
4. After cutting, apply a little cut paste into the wound and spread it out with the firm pressure of your thumb. Pasting will seal the cut and allow the wound to heal, decreasing the chance of disease in that area.

Fundamental Principles for Branch Selection

- Remove every single branch from the bottom 1/3 of the tree.
- Remove any limbs that hide or obscure the trunk's front.

- Do not allow two limbs to be the same height as in nature.
- Examine each limb and remove disproportionately thick ones from the top of the tree, keeping more expansive branches toward the bottom.
- Consider mature trees of the same species as your bonsai and imitate the spacing and quantity of main branches that occur naturally.
- Use a concave cutter to minimize the visibility of wounds and flaws caused by such drastic pruning.
- When pruning smaller branches, cut at a 45° angle, with the lowest point at the side opposite a bud on a branch (refer to illustration 2.0); this method encourages branching on deciduous trees. To achieve this on evergreens, remove young shoots to the point of another outward-facing branch.

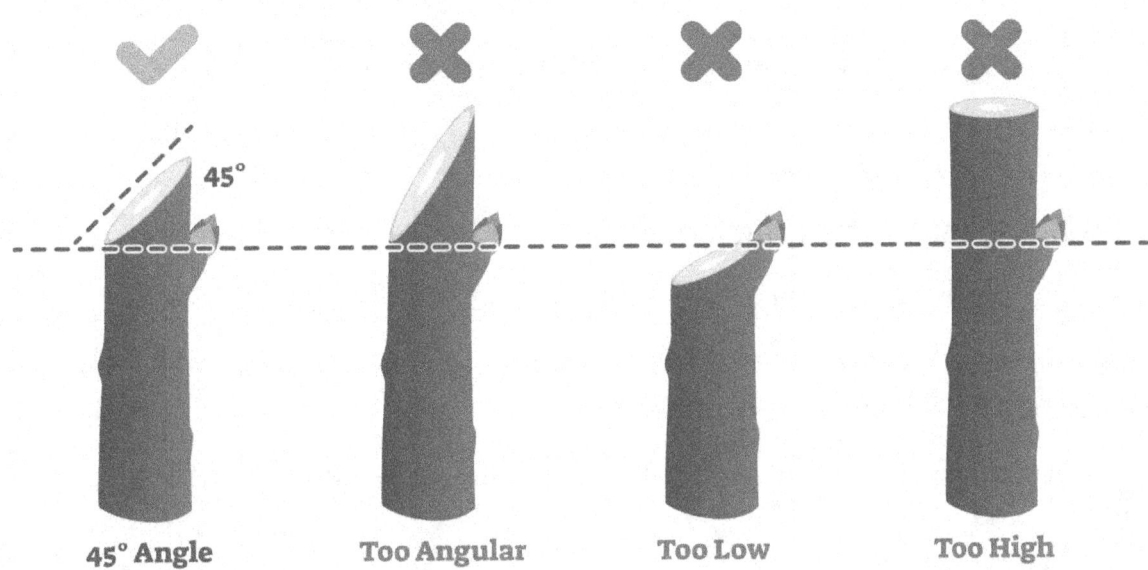

Illustration 2.0, the correct way to angle cut

Pruning large branches may leave unsightly scars, but as discussed above, using bonsai concave cutters can help to reduce scarring. Cut paste, available at most online Bonsai stores, helps protect the wounds and assists the tree in healing faster. Using the correct bonsai equipment will once again aid significantly.

After a tree has been styled, some people advocate cutting or eliminating an equal number of roots. A healthy tree can tolerate pruning up to a third of its foliage. However, most experts recommend performing one major maintenance at a time (or even once a year). For example, if you structure-prune this spring, you should postpone any repotting or root cutting until the following spring when the tree has recovered fully from the structure-pruning.

Maintenance pruning is done to older trees and is used to maintain the tree's shape. The first step in maintenance pruning is to remove any dead or dying branches. Maintenance pruning helps keep the tree healthy and free of disease. A concave cutter should remove dead branches close to the tree's trunk. Also, remove any branches growing in the wrong direction or are too large for the pot.

Proper pruning techniques can be complex and take years to master. However, there are a few basic rules that all beginners should follow:
- Always use sharp tools when pruning your bonsai tree. This will help reduce the risk of injury to the tree.
- When pruning, try to mimic the shape of the tree's natural growth pattern.
- On smaller branches, always make clean cuts just above a node (the point on a branch where a leaf or bud grows.) Take care not to damage the bark when pruning.
- Avoid pruning too much at one time. Prune a little bit every few weeks instead of trying to do it all at once.

Don't be afraid to experiment. Pruning is an art, and there is no one right way to do it.

How often should I prune my tree?

That depends on the type of tree, its age, and how vigorously it grows. Generally, most trees should be pruned once or twice a year. However, more mature trees may only need to be pruned yearly. Young trees may need to be pruned up to four times a year.

Wiring

Once you have pruned your tree into the desired shape, it's time to wire it. Wiring helps to give your tree its final form by bending and manipulating the trunk and branches.

When wiring, always use smooth, annealed copper or aluminum wire. Never use anything else as it can damage the tree.

In theory, most tree species may be wired at any time. However, different seasons have benefits and drawbacks for the bonsai and the stylist. Because many distinct tree kinds are created as bonsai and cultivated in diverse climatic environments, it's nearly impossible to provide a general rule. Many tiny cracks occur when the branches are forced into a new form in the bark and cambium layer. These injuries can mend easily and fast during the growing season. After a few weeks, the new branch position solidifies in deciduous trees. Outside of the growing season, this process takes much longer.

Step by Step Bonsai Wiring

1. **Examine your bonsai** and determine which branches require styling.
2. **Prepare your wiring** and select the appropriate wire size and length. A thicker wire will be required for larger branches and the trunk.
3. **Secure the wire.** Start by fixing one end of the bonsai wire in the ground or on the trunk. It would help to place the wire into the ground, with the end of the wire 1 - 1 1/2 inches into the soil behind the tree.
4. **Wire from strong to weak.** The wire is attached from the bottom up or starting from the interior to the tree's exterior, which means it's always going from the more robust to the less robust part of your bonsai. It may be wired clockwise or counterclockwise, depending on whether you want to bend it leftward or rightward.

5. **Wrapping.** Wrap the wire tight but without too much pressure to cut into the trunk or branch bark. Wrap the wire at 45° angles all the way along until the wire has covered all branches required for bending.

6. **Hold a branch securely** with your fingers, and gently bend the wired branch into the desired position. Keep your thumb pressed against the bend to offer support and reduce the risk of the branch breaking.

7. **Add gentle curves** to a limb to make it look more natural.

Image 4.0. Always start wiring from the main trunk or the largest branch and work outwards from the tree's center, wrapping each branch at 45° angles as shown in this image.

Important Points to Remember When Wiring:

- A single piece of wire may be used to train two adjacent branches. This adds more strength and stability to the branch.
- When you're ready to move on to the branch or branches you want to

shape, make sure the wire has been wrapped at least twice around the tree trunk.

- If you're bending down a branch, bring the wire up from beneath it. If wiring a limb upwards, begin above it.

Repotting

Generally, bonsai trees only need to be repotted every three years when their roots become pot-bound. When repotting, be sure to choose a pot that is only slightly larger than the current pot. Soak the soil in the pot for about an hour to soften the roots, then remove the plant from its container, making sure to gently ease the trunk to one side while removing from the old pot. Never pull the tree directly up as this may damage the larger roots. If the root ball is tightly compacted, use a blunt object such as chopsticks or your hand to break up the soil before planting.

Prune the long vertically spreading roots away; this replaces growth to the sideways-growing roots. As a result, these roots will thicken over time and form a natural Bonsai Nebari appearance. However, if you repot your plants regularly (every 2 - 3 years), trimming vertical roots should be sufficient to encourage surface root growth. When growing young material, some growers put their trees on a stone to force the tree to grow its roots sidewards. Continue cutting back the fine roots until the remaining root structure is 1/2 – 3/4 an inch smaller than the inside edge of the new pot. Do this to the root's depth as well.

3.0 Using bonsai scissors to trim away vertical growing roots before repotting is easy but essential, allowing the roots to grow sideways and outward to form a Nebari.

Next, cover the new pot's drainage hole with wire mesh just large enough to cover the hole, and use wire to secure it to the hole. The mesh will stop soil from falling out and aid with water drainage.

You will also want to anchor your bonsai to the new pot using thick gauge wire. Start by cutting a long piece and threading it through the wire mesh in the bottom of the pot to form a U-shape, leaving both wire ends sticking up out of the pot. Then cut off any excess wire and push it into the soil, hiding it from sight. When you have finished pruning the roots and are ready, place the tree in the new pot, and wrap the ends of the wire over the roots, twisting the ends together firmly over the root system. Similar to how you would wrap a present with string.

Finally, the bonsai should be planted at the same depth it was in its previous container. Use bonsai soil to fill the new pot and place the tree in the center. Gently backfill the hole with soil, being careful not to compact it. Water the tree twice and put it in a sunny spot.

What to keep in mind when repotting;

- **The best time to repot.** Early spring is the best time to repot when the climate starts to turn milder, between 46 - 50 °F (8 - 10 °C), and just before the buds on the tree begin to grow fully.
- **Signs of new growth.** In early spring, you will notice that tiny buds have started to form on the branches of your bonsai tree. This is the best time to repot, as the tree is still in its dormant stage and will not be as sensitive to the transplanting process.
- **The roots have filled the pot.** When the roots of your bonsai tree fill up the pot, it's time for a new pot. If you wait any longer, the roots will start to circle the pot and constrict the tree's growth. Start by carefully taking the tree out of its pot and pinching the soil with your fingers. There is no need to repot if the soil is soft and pliable and only a few roots show around the edge.
- **The pot is cracked or broken.** Do not try to fix the pot with tape or sealant, as this will only damage the tree's roots. If your pot is cracked or broken, it's time for a new pot.
- **The soil is compacted.** When the soil in your pot becomes compacted, it's time to repot. This can be caused by overwatering, so be sure to water your tree less often and allow the soil to dry out between waterings.

- **The tree has been recently transplanted.** If you have recently transplanted your tree, it's best to wait at least two growing seasons before repotting, even three in many instances. This will give the roots time to adjust to their new environment and become established.

In summary, pruning should be done to mimic the shape of the tree's natural growth pattern. Repotting should only be done every two to three years and only when the roots become pot-bound. Watering should be done regularly, but not too much, and the soil should be allowed to dry out between waterings. By following these simple maintenance techniques, you can ensure that your bonsai tree remains healthy and beautiful for many years to come

9 Top Tips for Ultimate Bonsai Care Mastery

Bonsai trees are delicate, and it's essential to handle them with care.

1. When you first buy your tree, your primary goal as its new caretaker is to **keep it alive**. Avoid any temptation to prune it straight away, as this may shock the tree and kill it. It is often best to wait until next spring before pruning. Your tree will thank you for doing so!
2. When repotting, be sure to use a pot that is the correct size for the tree. A pot that is too small can damage the roots and stunt the tree's growth.
3. If you buy an inexpensive bonsai, chances are it may need repotting straight away. These trees are often mass produced and before being sold, placed into a pot that may look wonderful but will likely be too small for the root system.
4. When watering, be sure to use room temperature water. Hot or cold water can shock the tree and damage the roots.
5. Be sure to fertilize your bonsai tree regularly, but in small amounts. Fertilizer helps the tree to grow healthy and strong.
6. When the tree is dormant in winter, it's essential to keep it in a cool, dark place. A warm room can damage the tree.
7. Pruning is an essential part of bonsai tree care, but it's also necessary to know when not to prune. Avoid pruning your bonsai tree during the winter, which can damage the tree. Winter is a time of rest for trees, and pruning can shock the tree and cause it to die.
8. Be sure to place your bonsai tree in a location that receives plenty of sunlight out of the winter months. A tree that doesn't get enough sunlight will not be able to produce food for itself and may slowly die.
9. When transporting your bonsai tree, always use a container designed to transport plants. A regular pot can easily break the roots of the tree.

By following these top tips, You will achieve peace of mind knowing that you are doing all there is to maintain a healthy and happy bonsai.

Chapter Six

COMMON PESTS AND DISEASES, AND HOW TO TREAT THEM

Bonsai trees are susceptible to a variety of pests and diseases. The most common include aphids, scale insects, spider mites, whiteflies, mealybugs, root rot, and powdery mildew. It's essential to check your tree regularly for signs of pests or disease. If you notice anything abnormal, treat the problem right away.

Aphids

Aphids are small, sap-sucking insects that can cause severe damage to bonsai trees. They can be challenging to see, as they are tiny and often hidden between the leaves. If you notice your tree is wilting or the leaves are turning yellow, you likely have an aphid infestation. To treat aphids, use a garden hose to spray them off the leaves, then treat them with insecticidal soap.

Scale Insects

Scale insects are tiny, sap-sucking insects that can cause severe damage to bonsai trees. They are easy to spot, as they look like small bumps on the branches or leaves. If you notice scale insects on your tree, use a cotton swab dipped in rubbing alcohol to remove them. Then, treat with insecticidal soap.

Spider Mites

Spider mites are tiny spider-like pests that can cause severe damage to bonsai trees. They are challenging to see, as they are small and often hidden between the leaves. If you notice your tree is wilting or the leaves are turning yellow, you likely have a spider mite infestation. To treat spider mites, use a garden hose to spray them off the leaves, then treat them with insecticidal soap.

Whiteflies

Whiteflies are small, sap-sucking insects that can cause severe damage to bonsai trees. They are easy to spot, as they look like tiny white moths flying around the leaves. If you notice whiteflies on your tree, use a garden hose to spray them off the leaves, then treat them with insecticidal soap.

Mealybugs

Mealybugs are tiny, sap-sucking insects that can cause severe damage to bonsai trees. They are easy to spot, as they look like tiny white insects covered in a waxy substance. If you notice mealybugs on your tree, use a cotton swab dipped in rubbing alcohol to remove them. Then, treat with insecticidal soap.

Caterpillars

Caterpillars are small, green insects that can cause severe damage to bonsai trees. They are easy to spot, as they often hide in the leaves. If you notice caterpillars on your tree, use a garden hose to spray them off the leaves, then treat them with insecticidal soap.

Root Rot

Root rot is a severe problem that can kill bonsai trees. It's caused by a fungus that attacks the roots, causing them to rot. If you notice your tree is wilting or the leaves are turning yellow, you likely have root rot. Remove the tree from the pot and rinse the roots with clean water to treat root rot. Then, replant in fresh bonsai soil and water well.

Powdery Mildew

Powdery mildew is a fungus that can cause severe damage to bonsai trees. It's easy to spot, as it looks like a white powder on the leaves and stems. If you notice powdery mildew on your tree, treat it with a fungicide.

Bacterial Leaf Scorch

Bacterial leaf scorch is a severe disease that can kill bonsai trees. It's caused by bacteria that attack the leaves, causing them to turn yellow and wilt. If you notice your tree is wilting or the leaves turn yellow, you likely have bacterial leaf scorch. To treat bacterial leaf scorch, remove the tree from the pot and rinse the leaves with clean water. Then, treat with antibiotics. Bonsai antibiotics are available from bonsai nurseries.

Fungal Leaf Spot

Fungal leaf spot is a type of fungus that can cause severe damage to bonsai trees. It's easy to spot, as it looks like tiny brown spots on the leaves. If you notice a fungal leaf spot on your tree, treat it with a fungicide.

Bacterial Blight

Bacterial blight is a severe disease that can kill bonsai trees. It's caused by bacteria that attack the leaves, causing them to turn brown and wilt. If you notice your tree is wilting or the leaves are turning brown, you likely have bacterial blight. Remove the tree from the pot and rinse the leaves with clean water to treat bacterial blight. Then, treat with antibiotics. Bonsai antibiotics are available from bonsai nurseries.

Pests and diseases can be a severe problem for bonsai trees. If you notice any pests or diseases on your tree, it's essential to treat them immediately.

Chapter Seven

CREATIVE TRIMMING AND PRUNING

Bonsai trees can be trimmed and pruned into various shapes and styles. To achieve a specific kind, you'll need to trim regularly, shape, and prune your tree. The following are 14 styles to spark your interest in truly getting creative with your first bonsai. These styles include:

Formal Upright Style (Chokkan)

Informal Upright Style (Moyogi)

Slanting Style (Shakan)

Cascade Style (Kengai)

Semi Cascade Style (Han-kengai)

Literati Style (Bunjingi)

Broom Style (Hokidachi)

Windswept Style (Fukinagashi)

Double Trunk Style (Sokan)

Multi-trunk Style (Kabudachi)

Forest Style (Yose-ue)

Growing on a Rock Style (Seki-joju)

Raft Style (Ikadabuki)

Shari Style (Sharimiki)

Formal Upright Style (Chokkan)

The Chokkan bonsai style is the most formal upright style. It is often used for plants that are indigenous to the area, such as pines, junipers, and maples. A straight trunk characterizes this style, and the leaves should be placed evenly along the branches. The leaves should be slightly larger than leaves in other styles.

The Chokkan style originated in Japan during the Edo period. It was used to display plants that were native to the area, and it quickly became popular among bonsai enthusiasts. This style often occurs in nature, especially when a tree is trying to reach the sunlight. The tree's apex will be pointing upwards, and the roots will be visible.

The formal upright style is the most popular style for bonsai trees. It involves trimming the tree into a tall, narrow shape with a symmetrical canopy. To create a formal upright style bonsai, you'll need to trim the tree regularly. You'll also need to prune the roots to keep them small and compact.

Formal Upright Style (Chokkan)

Informal Upright Style (Moyogi)

The Moyogi bonsai style originated from the Edo period in Japan. It is the most common type of bonsai, and it can be used for various plants. The informal upright style is typical in the wild and the art of bonsai. The trunk grows in an upright fashion; however, it will be curved rather than straight. This curve can be either S-shaped or windswept. The branches will also be asymmetrical, and the tree's apex will point upwards.

The informal upright style is similar to the formal upright style but with a few key differences. The most obvious difference is that the trunk is curved rather than straight. This gives the tree a more natural look. The branches are also asymmetrical, and the tree's apex points upwards.

To create an informal upright style bonsai, you'll need to trim the tree regularly. It involves trimming the tree into a tall, narrow shape but with a less symmetrical canopy. The branches should be unevenly spaced and point in different directions.

You won't need to prune the roots, but you should keep them trimmed and compact.

Informal Upright Style (Moyogi)

Slanting Style (Shakan)

The Shakan bonsai style was first seen in the late 1800s in Japan. It is used for plants that have a strong inclination to grow sideways. The slanting type is often used for bonsai trees with a broad base and a thin top. The trunk will be angled, and the branches will grow at a 45-degree angle. The slanting style is often used when a tree leans because of the wind blowing in one particular direction or when a tree grows in the shade and must bend toward the sun; it will lean in one direction. The leaning style should grow at a 45-60 degree angle from the soil with bonsai.

The slanting style is created by trimming the tree into a tall, narrow shape that leans to one side. The branches should be evenly spaced and pointing in different directions.

To create a slanting style bonsai, you'll need to trim the tree regularly and use wiring to help shape the branches. You should also keep the roots trimmed and compact.

Slanting Style (Shakan)

Cascade Style (Kengai)

This style imitates a tree living in nature that bends downwards, often due to the weight of the snow or falling rocks, and often hanging off a cliff. The cascade style should hang down two-thirds the height of the tree and must be able to support its weight.

The cascade style is created by trimming the tree into a tall, narrow shape that hangs downwards. The branches should be evenly spaced and pointing in different directions.

To create a cascade-style bonsai, you'll need to trim the tree regularly. The tree must be able to support its weight, so it's essential to make sure the trunk is strong. It would help if you also pruned the roots to keep them small and compact.

Cascade Style (Kengai)

Semi Cascade Style (Han-kengai)

The Han-kengai bonsai is similar to the cascade style, but the tree is not allowed to hang below the pot. This style is often used for trees with a weeping or cascading growth habit and is found in the wild clinging precariously to cliffs or over the banks of lakes and rivers. The tree branches are trained to grow downwards, often with long internodes between the branches.

When styling a tree in the Han-kengai style, the most crucial consideration is to ensure that the branches grow downwards and not outwards. You can achieve this by wiring the branches and training them into the desired position.

The Han-kengai style is a popular choice for bonsai enthusiasts, as it can create an exquisite and graceful tree. It is important to remember that this style takes a long time to perfect, and it is not suitable for all tree species. If you consider creating a bonsai in the Han-kengai style, it is important to choose a tree with a naturally cascading growth habit. Some of the most popular species for this style include juniper, azalea, and elm.

Semi Cascade Style (Han-kengai)

Literati Style (Bunjingi)

The literati style is characterized by a thin trunk, often with only a few branches. The leaves are small, and the tree's overall shape is slender and elegant. In nature, this tree style is found in areas where the soil is poor, and the tree must struggle to survive.

The literati style is created by trimming the tree into a tall, slender shape with only a small canopy. The leaves should be small, and the branches should be evenly spaced.

To create a literati-style bonsai, you'll need to trim the tree regularly. The tree must be able to support its weight, so it's essential to make sure the trunk is strong. It would be best if you also pruned the roots to keep them small and compact.

Literati Style (Bunjingi)

Broom Style (Hokidachi)

This style is used for trees with a wide, flat top and a thin trunk. The branches will grow outwards from the trunk in all directions, creating a broad canopy.

The broom style is often used for trees repotted in a shallow pot, as it gives the tree a more natural appearance.

When styling a tree in the broom style, the most crucial consideration is to ensure that the branches are evenly spaced and pointing in different directions. You can achieve this by wiring the branches and training them into the desired position.

The broom style is a popular choice for bonsai enthusiasts, as it can create a beautiful and graceful tree. It is important to remember that this style takes a long time to perfect, and it is not suitable for all tree species.

Choosing a tree with a naturally broad growth habit is vital if you consider creating a bonsai in the broom style. Some of the most popular species for this style include elm, maple, and oak.

Broom Style (Hokidachi)

Windswept Style (Fukinagashi)

This style is used for trees with a thin trunk and long, sweeping branches. The overall shape of the tree should resemble a windblown tree in nature. The windswept style is created by wiring the branches and training them into the desired position.

The windswept style is a popular choice for bonsai enthusiasts, as it can create a magnificent and graceful tree. It is important to remember that this style takes a long time to perfect, and it is not suitable for all tree species.

If you are considering creating a bonsai in the windswept style, it is vital to choose a tree that has a naturally thin growth habit. Some of the most popular species for this style include elm, maple, and oak.

This style is ideal for trees with a long, thin trunk and few branches. A narrow canopy will be formed as the branches grow outwards from the trunk in one direction.

The windswept style is often used for trees repotted in a shallow pot, as it gives the tree a more natural appearance.

When designing a tree in the windswept style, keep in mind that the branches should be evenly spaced and pointing in the same direction. You can achieve this by wiring the branches and training them into the desired position.

It is important to remember that this style takes a long time to perfect, and it is not suitable for all tree species.

If you are considering creating a bonsai in the windswept style, it is essential to choose a tree that has a naturally long, slender growth habit. Some of the most popular species for this style include elm, maple, and oak.

Windswept Style (Fukinagashi)

Double Trunk Style (Sokan)

One of the most classic and elegant bonsai styles is the double trunk or sokan. In this style, two trunks emerge from a single root system and grow parallel to one another. The trunks may be of unequal size, but they should be approximately the same length.

The branches on each trunk should also be roughly equal in size, and the foliage should be symmetrical on both trunks. This style is often used with conifers, but deciduous trees can also be used.

There are a few things to keep in mind when styling a tree in the double trunk style:

1. Make sure that the two trunks are of relatively equal thickness. If one trunk is significantly thicker than the other, it will look out of proportion.
2. The trunks should taper evenly from the base to the top.
3. The branches on each trunk should be arranged to be pleasing to the eye.

One of the challenges of this style is keeping the two trunks evenly balanced. This can be difficult, especially if the tree is not symmetrical. It is essential to carefully consider the placement of each branch and leaves so that the tree looks balanced overall.

The double trunk style is a classic bonsai style that can be challenging to master.

Double Trunk Style (Sokan)

Multi-trunk Style (Kabudachi)

The Kabudachi style, also known as the multi-trunk style, is one of the most popular bonsai styles. This style features multiple trunks that emerge from a single point or root system. The trunks can be of different thicknesses and lengths, and they may branch out in different directions. The branches are often arranged symmetrically, and the leaves are typically small and neat.

The Kabudachi style is often used to create dramatic or formal bonsai trees. It can be used to showcase the beauty of a single tree species, or it can be used to show off the diversity of a forest scene. The multi-trunk style is also well-suited for creating bonsai trees with a strong visual impact.

If you're looking to create a bonsai tree in the Kabudachi style, choosing a well-suited species for this type of treatment is crucial.

Multi-trunk Style (Kabudachi)

Forest Style (Yose-ue)

This style features multiple trees planted close together in a single pot. The trees can be of different sizes. The branches of each tree should be arranged to create a pleasing composition, and the leaves should be small and neat.

The forest style is often used to create dramatic or informal bonsai trees. It can be used to showcase the beauty of a single tree species, or it can be used to show off the diversity of a forest scene. The forest style is also well-suited for creating bonsai trees with a strong visual impact.

Forest Style (Yose-ue)

Growing on a Rock Style (Seki-joju)

Bonsai on a rock is a unique style of bonsai that can be very difficult to master. The tree needs to be carefully trained to grow in the limited space on the rock, and it takes a lot of time and effort to keep the tree healthy and looking good. However, this style can be awe-inspiring and add interest to any bonsai collection when done correctly.

There are several different ways to grow a tree on a rock. One popular method is to use a pre-made rock or driftwood with holes drilled and then wire the tree in place. Alternatively, you can use a natural rock, which can be a little more challenging and more rewarding. The most important thing is to ensure that the rock is stable and will not move around; otherwise, the tree can quickly become damaged or die.

The best trees for this style are deciduous trees since they have robust root systems that can withstand the limited growing space. Conifers are not well suited for this style as they tend to have shallow root systems that can easily be damaged. Some of the best trees for this style include maples, oaks, and elms.

Once you have chosen the right tree and rock, it is time to start training the tree. This can be done by carefully bending and shaping the branches to create the desired shape. It is important to be very careful when doing this, as it is easy to damage the tree if you are not careful. Once the tree has been trained into the desired shape, it will need to be wired in place to stay in that position.

Once the tree is in place, you will need to water it regularly and fertilize it to stay healthy. Bonsai on a rock can be a bit more challenging to care for than other bonsai styles, but as long as you are careful and give the tree the attention it needs, it should do just fine.

Growing on a Rock Style (Seki-joju)

Raft Style (Ikadabuki)

This is a unique style of bonsai in which the tree is growing out of a hollowed-out log or piece of driftwood. The roots are exposed, and the tree is often styled to look like it's clinging to its precarious perch.

Raft-style bonsai are often created with fast-growing tree species like elm, cedar, and juniper. The tree will quickly consume the driftwood or log, making a natural bonsai pot.

The raft style is popular for beginner bonsai enthusiasts because it is relatively easy to create without special tools or materials.

If you're interested in creating a raft-style bonsai, we recommend starting with a fast-growing tree species such as elm, cedar, or juniper. Once you've selected your tree, simply hollow out a log or piece of driftwood and plant your tree inside.

Raft Style (Ikadabuki)

Shari Style (Sharimiki)

The shari style is popular for enthusiasts who want to create a bonsai with an aged and weathered look. The tree is usually planted in a pot that has been carved to resemble a dead trunk, and the branches are styled to look like they are growing out of decaying wood.

Shari-style bonsai are often created with slow-growing tree species such as pine and fir. This is because it can take many years for the tree to achieve the desired aged appearance.

The shari style is a popular choice for intermediate bonsai enthusiasts because it requires some basic carving skills and patience.

If you're interested in creating a shari-style bonsai, we recommend starting with a slow-growing tree species such as pine or fir. Once you've selected your tree, carve a pot to resemble a dead trunk and plant your tree inside.

Shari Style (Sharimiki)

Once you've taken all of these factors into consideration, you should have a good idea of what type of bonsai tree you'd like to grow. If you're still unsure, I recommend checking the Best Bonsai Trees for Beginners list, covered earlier in Chapter Three.

Chapter Eight

NEXT LEVEL BONSAI

Summer Care

Undoubtedly, summers are becoming longer and hotter due to climate change, which can impact your bonsai on many levels. The main thing to remember is to keep an eye on your trees' watering and feeding requirements.

Potted trees build up considerable heat, and a lack of moisture will quickly dry out the delicate roots. If you're going on vacation, have someone check on your bonsai at least once a week, or consider installing an automated watering system like the Blumat or Gardena Microdrip as discussed in Chapter Five; under 'Watering.'

Azaleas require special care in July. They are susceptible to sunburn, so make sure they get enough shade.

Summer is also the time to monitor your styled trees' shari and jin portions. Shari is the white deadwood area on a tree, and jin is the deadwood with living bark. Exposure to the sun can cause these areas to crack, so make sure they're well-protected.

In general, be careful not to over-expose your bonsai to the sun. This can cause them to dry out and lose their leaves. Keep an eye on the weather report, and give your trees a break from the sun when it's too hot.

11 Advanced Techniques for the Bonsai Gardener

If you want to grow bonsai trees to an expert level, these are some techniques you'll need to master;

1. **Thicken Your Bonsai Tree's Trunk.** To do this, allow your bonsai to grow taller before you prune it back. When you prune it, cut back to just above a set of leaves. This will give your tree more character and make it look older. Thickening your bonsai may take several years, but it is well worth waiting.

2. **Create Branch Taper.** Bonsai trees have a natural look of being wider at the bottom and narrower at the top. To achieve this, you will need to prune your branches strategically. The best time to do this is in the spring or summer.

3. **Use Branch Chopsticks.** These are small pieces of wood that you can use to support branches while they grow. Place the branch chopsticks at the end of the branch and then tie them in place with wire. This will help to create a more natural look.

4. **Develop a Nebari.** A good nebari is an essential part of bonsai aesthetics. This is the visible root system of the tree. To develop a nebari, you will need to encourage the roots to grow outward. A nebari can be achieved by following two methods, air-layering or regularly pruning downward growing roots.

5. **Create Jin and Shari.** These are features that give your bonsai an aged look. To create deadwood, you will need to carefully remove the bark from the branches or roots of your tree using pliers. Jin is the bare stripped part on a branch, while Shari is the barkless part of a trunk. Deadwood features require some advanced tools. Invest in a pair of pruning shears, a concave cutter, pliers, and a wire saw to create the perfect Jin and Shari on your bonsai. This practice is best done in the spring or summer.

6. **Create a Windswept Look.** This is a popular style for bonsai trees. To create a windswept look, you will need to prune the branches to angle away from the trunk. This will give the impression that the wind has

blown the tree.

7. **Create a Moss Garden.** Moss is a great way to add color and texture to your bonsai tree. It also helps to keep the soil moist. You can buy moss online or at a garden center. When laying moss around your bonsai, make sure to leave room for the tree to grow.

8. **Create a Bonsai Pot Garden.** This is a great way to show off your bonsai trees. You can find bonsai pot gardens online or at a specialty bonsai store. You will need a variety of pots in different sizes and shapes.

9. **Shape Your Bonsai Tree Using Training Wires.** The art of shaping your bonsai with training wires is called training. These are used to shape your bonsai tree. Different training wires are available, so choose the right ones for your tree.

10. **Soak Your Bonsai Tree.** This is a great way to hydrate your tree and keep it healthy. It is also an excellent way to remove any pests or diseases on your tree. To soak your bonsai, place it in a water container and allow it to sit for several hours. Be sure to change the water regularly.

11. **Defoliate Your Bonsai Tree.** This is a technique that is used to encourage new growth. To defoliate your bonsai, you will need to remove all of the leaves from the tree. You can do this by hand or with a pair of scissors. Be sure only to remove the leaves and not the stems. The best time to defoliate your tree is in the spring or summer.

With a bit of creativity, you can create a genuinely stunning tree. These are just a few of the techniques that experts use. With time and practice, you can create a work of art.

5 Beginner Mistakes to Avoid

When it comes to bonsai, there are a few things you should avoid doing to ensure your tree's health. Below are some common mistakes that beginners make:

1. **Overwatering.** One of the most common mistakes made by beginners is overwatering their bonsai tree. Overwatering can quickly lead to root rot, which will kill the tree. Bonsai trees only need watering when the top inch of soil feels dry to the touch.

2. **Underwatering.** Another common mistake is not watering the tree enough, which can cause the leaves to wilt and the tree to die. Bonsai trees need water when the top inch of soil feels dry to the touch, but be careful not to overwater.

3. **Fertilizing.** Fertilizing too often or using the wrong type of fertilizer is another common mistake. Using too much fertilizer can damage the roots and cause the tree to die. Bonsai trees only need fertilizing once a month, and you should use a fertilizer made explicitly for bonsai trees.

4. **Pruning.** Another common mistake is pruning the tree too often or removing the wrong branches. Over pruning can stunt a tree's growth and cause it to die. Prune the tree only when necessary, and be sure to remove the correct branches.

5. **Repotting.** Another common mistake is repotting the tree too often or not repotting it when necessary. Inappropriately repotting can damage the roots and cause the tree to die. Only repot the tree when necessary, and be sure to use a pot that is only slightly larger than the current one.

Avoiding these five beginner mistakes when growing your bonsai will ensure the health and longevity of your tree.

Chapter Nine

FREQUENTLY ASKED QUESTIONS

How do I choose a bonsai tree?
There is no specific answer to this question as each person's preference will be different. You may want to consider the tree species, the size, and the shape when making your selection. Please refer to Chapter Three, "Best Bonsai Trees for Beginners," with suggestions on choosing the best tree when starting your bonsai journey.

What kind of soil should I use for my bonsai tree?
Bonsai soil is different from regular potting soil as it must provide good drainage while still retaining moisture. Never use regular potting soil for these reasons. Many commercially available bonsai soils will work well, or you can make your own mix using ingredients such as bark, peat moss, and perlite.

How often should I water my bonsai tree?
This will vary depending on the type of tree, the climate, and the potting mix. Generally, bonsai trees should be watered every other day or once a week in winter. If the soil is still moist, refrain from watering.

How often should I fertilize my bonsai tree?

Fertilizing a bonsai tree is vital for ensuring its health and vitality. You may choose to reduce the suggested amount for trees that are no longer in training to balance their development rather than stimulate it. When using solid fertilizer, you should use fertilizer covers to keep the nutrients in place. Overfeeding your trees may have severe consequences for their health, so don't go overboard.

What is the best way to prune my bonsai tree?

Pruning a bonsai tree is essential for keeping its shape and size under control. When pruning, use good quality, sharp scissors and sharp concave cutters. And as my grandfather used to say, "less is more." You can always prune more another day.

My tree is losing its leaves. What is wrong?

It is important to remember that deciduous bonsai trees will lose their leaves in the fall, so this should not cause alarm. Leaves falling off a bonsai tree can be due to several factors, such as overwatering, underwatering, poor soil, or pests and diseases. If you are unsure what is causing your tree to lose its leaves, it is best to consult with an expert.

Can I keep my bonsai tree outdoors?

Most bonsai trees can be kept outdoors, but there are a few exceptions. Some bonsai species, such as the Ficus, will not survive if kept outdoors in cold weather.

I'm having trouble keeping my bonsai tree healthy. What should I do?

If you are having difficulty keeping your bonsai tree healthy, it is best to consult with an expert. Take your bonsai to a local nursery that specializes in bonsai if possible. They will be able to help you identify the problem and provide solutions.

Conclusion

Bonsai trees are a type of plant that can often be misunderstood. Many people believe that they are challenging to care for when all they require is a bit of extra attention. A bonsai tree can bring peace and beauty to your home for many years with the proper care.

If you're thinking about starting your bonsai journey, be sure to do your research and choose a tree that is well suited for beginners. Once you have your tree, water it regularly, fertilize it monthly and prune it only when necessary.

Now that you have finished reading this book, you should understand the basics of bonsai. You should know how to select and care for a tree, shape it, and pot it. You should also be familiar with some of the most common bonsai styles. Of course, this is just the beginning. With care and attention, your bonsai tree will be a beautiful addition to your home for years to come.

I love bonsai because it forces me to slow down and be present. I love bonsai for its ability to calm me when my thoughts are scattered, and its beauty helps me appreciate the circle of life. Bonsai reminds me that some things are worth waiting for and that the best things in life often take time, effort, and patience to achieve. And most importantly, it reminds me of my grandfather, who first introduced me to this beautiful art form.

Remember, the best bonsai are not created overnight—they are the result of years of patience, practice, and love.

I hope you will come to love the art of bonsai and will take up the challenge of growing your own. Remember to start small, be patient, and be prepared to make mistakes – it's all part of the learning process. With time and practice, you will become a Master of Bonsai.

Please Consider Leaving a Review

If you have enjoyed reading this book and found it helpful, it would mean wonders to me if you left a favorable review for the book on Amazon. Also, reviewing my book helps it get recognized on Amazon by more bonsai enthusiasts, and in turn, I hope it will help them with their own bonsai journey.

The Easy Way

Scan the QR code below to be taken directly to your Amazon Purchase Review page. From there, it's a quick and easy way to leave a written review for **Bonsai for Beginners**.

Thank you and best wishes,
Ron Sakai

Resources

- "Bonsai Styles." *Bonsai Empire*, www.bonsaiempire.com/origin/bonsai-styles. Accessed 18 May 2022.

Chan, Peter. *The Bonsai Beginner's Bible.* Illustrated, Mitchell Beazley, 2018.

Lesniewicz, Paul. *Indoor Bonsai.* 1994 Reprint, Kindle ed., Cassell Illustrated, 1986.

Lewis, Colin. Bonsai Basics - A Comprehensive Guide to Care and Cultivation: A Pyramid Paperback (Pyramid Gardening (Paperback)). Illustrated, Hamlyn, 2009.

Lewis, Colin, and Jack Douthitt. *Bonsai Survival Manual: Tree-by-Tree Guide to Buying, Maintaining, and Problem Solving.* Later Printing, Storey Publishing, LLC, 1996.

Lofgren, Kristine. "PRUNING BONSAI 101: HOW TO SHAPE YOUR PLANTS." *Gardener's Path*, 7 Dec. 2021, gardenerspath.com/plants/ornamentals/pruning-bonsai.

Nakamura, Asashi. "Bonsai Tree Styles." *Bonsai Tree Gardener*, 2 Oct. 2018, www.bonsaitreegardener.net/bonsai-trees/styles.

Tomlinson, Harry. *The Complete Book of Bonsai: A Practical Guide to Its Art and Cultivation*. Abbeville Press, 1990.

"Wiring Bonsai." *BONSAISCHULE WENDDORF*, www.bonsai-shop.com/en/styling/wiring. Accessed 20 May 2022.

www.ingramcontent.com/pod-product-compliance
Lightning Source LLC
Chambersburg PA
CBHW081620100526
44590CB00021B/3533